FAVOURITE FLOWERS
in Ribbons and Threads

FAVOURITE FLOWERS
in Ribbons and Threads

Heather Joynes

Kangaroo Press

Acknowledgments

My grateful thanks to
- My husband Jack for his help and patience while I was writing this book.
- Cotton-on Creations (Suite 107, 2 Pembroke Street, Epping NSW 2121) for supplying the Kanagawa silk ribbons and threads.
- DMC Needlecraft Pty Ltd (55 Carrington Street, Marrickville NSW 2204) for supplying stranded and perle threads.

First published in 1996 by Kangaroo Press Pty Ltd
3 Whitehall Road Kenthurst NSW 2156 Australia
PO Box 6125 Dural Delivery Centre NSW 2158
Printed in Hong Kong through Colorcraft Ltd

ISBN 0 86417 754 2

Contents

Introduction

Choosing flowers for this book was not easy. There are so many beautiful ones that would translate well into embroidery with ribbons and threads. Eventually I settled on the seasons as the basis for selection. There are three flowers from each season with a project for each flower. There is also an arrangement using the three flowers together.

Most projects are worked in ribbons with stitchery in threads added; the others are worked purely in threads. Sometimes the flowers in the combined arrangement are worked differently from those in the main flower project. This gives a variety of techniques and designs. The projects include a number that are suitable for useful items, as well as several purely decorative pictures.

The embroidery is simple, with stitches that are easy to work. Readers are encouraged to add their own personal touches to the embroidery, to change the colours, interchange the designs and to develop their own ideas and designs to embroider.

Most flowers can be translated into embroidery. Study the plant carefully; take photographs and make drawings, preferably from life. The translation into embroidery requires some knowledge of stitches, but this will come gradually with the experience of stitching some of the flowers in this book.

Materials and equipment used in ribbon embroidery

Materials and Equipment

Fabric for ribbon embroidery should be firm. Velveteen, velvet, linen, polyester, cotton, silk and wool are all suitable provided they are firmly woven. If you are using a fine soft silk, back it with organza to give it more body.

The range of ribbons today is vast. Silk, polyester, velvet, satin and nylon are all available in lovely colours. Using velvet ribbon needs careful thought as it is hard to pull through fabric; it is best used on the surface of the fabric.

When you are buying ribbons with no specific purpose in mind (those you just can't resist) you will find that 2 metres (2 yards) is a useful quantity.

Ribbons are best wound onto cardboard thread winders, which can be kept in plastic thread boxes.

Tapestry and chenille needles in several sizes are essential, as also are crewel and straw needles in a variety of sizes.

There are many beautiful embroidery threads available in cotton, silk and rayon, some shaded. The most useful are the stranded cottons and perle cotton in Nos 5 and 8.

Other necessities are embroidery scissors and a larger pair of fabric scissors, embroidery hoops and frames and a stiletto or awl.

General Hints

- When stitching with silk ribbon, thread the ribbon into the needle then pass the point of the needle through one end of the ribbon and pull taut; this prevents the ribbon continually slipping out of the needle. This technique is not practical with satin ribbons, however, as it makes the ribbon hard to pull through the fabric.
- Use short lengths of ribbon, about 20 cm (8").
- To start, pull the ribbon through from the back, leaving an end of about 5 mm (¼"). When the embroidery is completed, sew the starting ends of the ribbon down with sewing cotton or one strand of stranded cotton.
- Finish the ribbon in the same way.
- Polyester satin ribbons need to be sewn down as soon as possible as they are very springy.
- Any embroidery that is to be worn or is to be washed should be sewn down very firmly.
- If it is difficult to pull a ribbon through a fabric, make a small hole with a stiletto or awl.

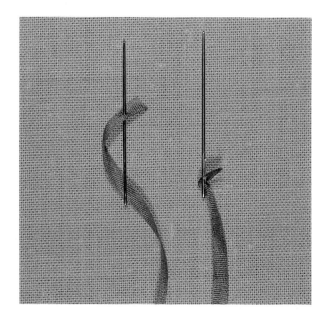

Needle threaded with ribbon

- Do not leave long ends of ribbon or thread at the back of the work, as they are likely to get tangled and cause difficulties.
- When pulling a ribbon through to the back of the work check to ensure that the needle is not piercing a ribbon already worked; if this happens it is difficult to pull the ribbon through and also distorts the work.
- Never leave embroidery in a hoop when you are not working on it, as the hoop marks will be hard to remove.

Designing

The design must be suitable in scale for the article you are making. Always establish the size and shape of the article first, then the area to be embroidered, then the details of the design. Details of the design can be kept very simple: using just circles and ovals for flowers and leaves, for example.

Designing for clothing needs special care as the whole garment has to be considered as well as the person who will wear it. Cut an extra paper pattern and mark on it the area to be embroidered, then try it against the person for whom the garment is intended. Any adjustments can be made before working up the design for the embroidery.

If it is an important garment it is worth making a calico replica (toile) with the design marked on it. Time spent planning and designing is time well spent which can save hours of anguish and unpicking. When working on anything with seams that will run through the embroidery, work on each piece of the article to within 3 cm (1") of the seam, sew up the seam, press on the wrong side, then complete the embroidery over the seam.

Transferring Designs

Only the bare essentials of the design need be transferred to the fabric to be embroidered. For small pieces, dots for the centres of the flowers and perhaps stem lines are all that is necessary. This is why it is important to work out the design first. It is not hard to follow a small design freehand.

Where a light coloured fabric is being used it is often possible to see the design through the fabric so that it can be traced with a quilter's pencil or sharp HB pencil.

For velvets or dark fabrics, trace the design onto tissue paper or baking paper. Pin the paper to the fabric and baste along the lines of the design in white cotton using small stitches. Tear away the paper, leaving the design outlined in basting

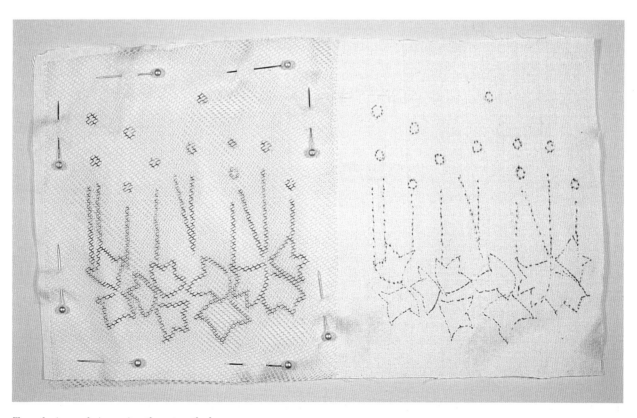

Transferring a design using the net method

stitches. These can be removed once the embroidery is completed.

Another method, for larger designs, is to trace the design onto nylon net with a black felt pen. Make sure both the design and the net are taped or weighted to the table to prevent slipping. Remove the net and pin it in place on the fabric, then go over the design with a water-soluble pen or sharp pencil. When you remove the net the design will appear on the fabric as a series of dots. The dots can be removed if they show after the embroidery is finished by holding a dampened cotton bud against them.

When transferring a design from a book by this method place a piece of firm clear plastic over the book before tracing over the design with a felt pen. This prevents the ink bleeding through the tracing paper onto the book.

Try to ensure that any marks made on the fabric will be covered by the embroidery.

Finishing

Your finished embroidery can be pressed lightly on the wrong side into a well padded surface. A folded towel is ideal. Take care not to flatten the embroidery. The marks made by embroidery hoops can usually be removed by damping the area with a light spray of water.

When mounting pictures make sure the mount is perfectly squared at the corners. If possible use acid-free board.

When working with glue, work over clean scrap paper—white is best, not newspaper. Change the paper at every stage of construction.

Stitches

Back Stitch

Back stitch can be used to outline flower petals, leaves and stems.

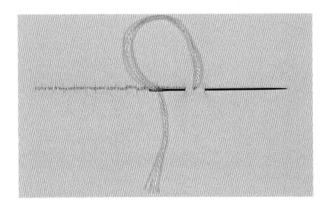

Bullion Knot

Use a straw needle for this stitch. Make a stitch as shown with the eye of the needle nearly into the fabric. Wind the thread around the needle as many times as will cover the length of the first stitch. Pull the needle and thread through the twists, holding the twists firmly with one hand. Take the needle down as shown. Makes good stamens.

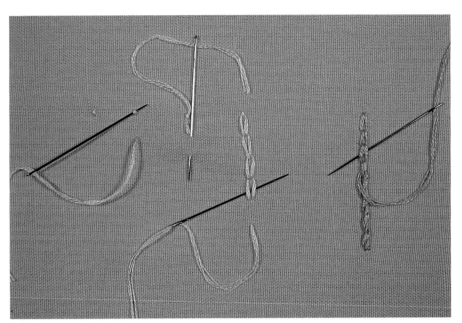

Chain Stitch Worked in a Frame

Make a small stitch, bringing the needle up below it for the required length of the chain stitch. Pass the needle under the small stitch (not through the fabric) and insert into the fabric where the needle emerged. Bring the needle up, again the length of a stitch, and pass needle and thread under the previous stitch, then continue in the same way.

For **whipped chain stitch** work a row of chain stitch first, then pass the needle and thread under each stitch, pulling the thread fairly taut. This makes a firm, rather raised line, good for stems.

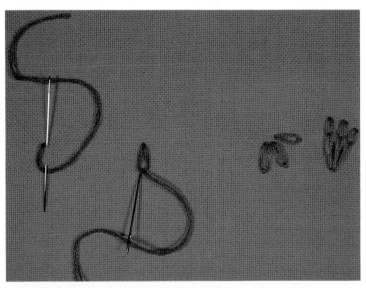

Detached Chain

This stitch is very useful for petals, buds and leaves. The tail of the stitch can be varied for different effects.

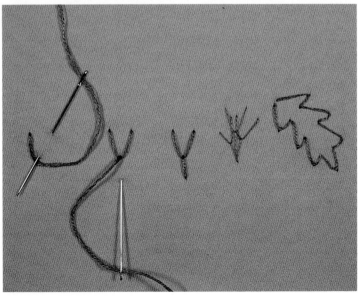

Fly Stitch

A most useful stitch that can be varied by altering the length of the tail or by making the stitch uneven.

French Knot

It is important to make only one twist around the needle, then pull through, holding the twist in finger and thumb. The knot should be snug against the fabric. Insert the needle near the starting point. French knots in ribbon need to be a little looser than in thread.

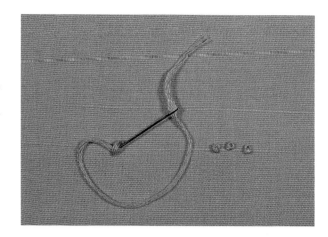

Herringbone Stitch

This stitch is good for attaching ribbons, particularly satin ribbon, and will take a curve well.

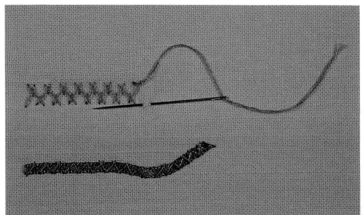

Running Stitch

Used to make a broken line down the centres of leaves, or to make a soft outline.

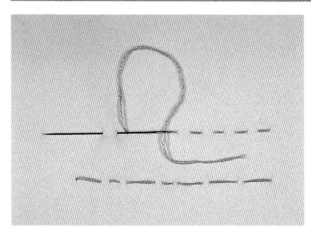

Satin Stitch

This is a difficult stitch to get perfect, but worth persevering with. It is best worked with a single untwisted thread.

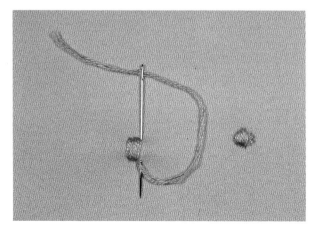

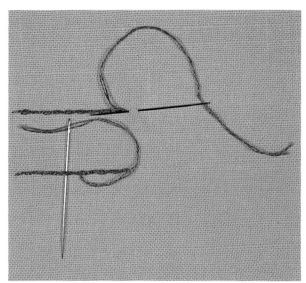

Stem Stitch

Unbeatable for smooth lines such as stems or outlines.

For **whipped stem stitch** pass the needle and thread under each stitch and pull taut. The right tension comes with experience.

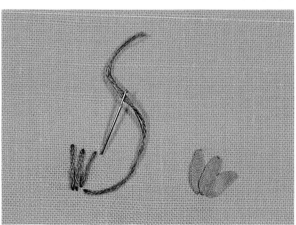

Straight Stitch

This stitch is used a great deal in ribbon embroidery for flower petals and leaves. It can be varied by making the stitch looser or tighter.

The Designs

SPRING

Crocus

You will need
4 mm silk ribbon in:
  yellow 16
  mauve 23
DMC stranded cotton in:
  yellow 741
  mauve 554
  greens 986, 987

Each petal of the flower is made with two straight stitches in silk ribbon. Work the outside petals first, then the centre one, which finishes a little below the outside petals.

With one strand of matching cotton, and using stem stitch, work a line starting about halfway up the outside of the flower and curving it around and down to form a stem. Work another line on the opposite side of the flower.

The leaves are worked in stem stitch, using two strands of stranded cotton, using mostly 986 with some leaves in 987.

Shirt and Belt Buckle

You will need
fabric for a plain shirt and belt (the shirt in the illustration is worked on a polyester/cotton)
2 m (2 yds) each of 4 mm silk ribbon in:
  mauve 23
  yellow 16
DMC stranded cotton in:
  yellow 741
  mauve 554
  greens 986, 987
length of belt backing, your waist size plus 20 cm (8")
piece of plastic 10 cm × 6 cm (4" × 2½") (ice-cream carton plastic is ideal)
10 cm (4") Velcro
thin batting 10 cm × 6 cm (4" × 2½")

Work the design on the pocket, which is then turned over and machine-stitched on the right side.

It should be possible to work the design from the diagram on page 16 without transferring the design to the fabric. The shirt can then be made up.

Crocus sampler

Opposite: Crocus shirt and belt buckle

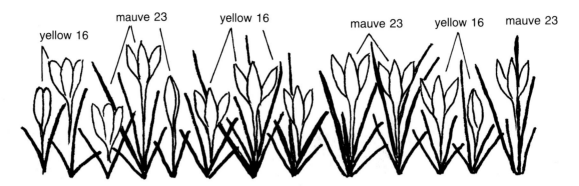

Shirt pocket

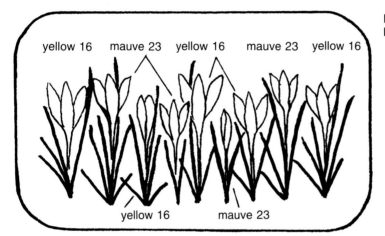

Flowers in straight stitches
Leaves and stems in stem stitch

Buckle

For the belt buckle, work the design on a piece of fabric 12 cm × 8 cm (5" × 3").

Cut the plastic to shape and glue a piece of batting to it.

Cover the plastic shape with the embroidered fabric and lace the fabric edges across the back to get a firm fit. Line with another piece of fabric with one side of the Velcro machine-stitched to it.

Make the belt and stitch the other side of the Velcro to one end. Overlap the buckle about 2.5 cm (1") on the other end and hand-stitch in place.

Daffodils

You will need
7 mm silk ribbon in:
  yellow 15
4 mm silk ribbon in:
  green 33
DMC stranded cotton in:
  yellow 725
  greens 522, 580

Each petal is a straight stitch in 7 mm ribbon. The trumpet is two petal stitches, one on top of the other, with the second stitch a little shorter than the first. The ends of the rolled part of the stitch are stitched down with a tiny stitch in matching cotton, bringing the ends of the ribbon stitches together.

The stems are worked in whipped stem stitch with three strands of green 522.

The leaves are long straight stitches in the green ribbon, stitched down the centre with running stitches in one strand of green 522. The grass below the daffodils is worked in straight stitches with two strands of green 580. (See next page.)

Needlecase

You will need
fabric 36 cm × 12 cm (14" × 5") (the fabric in the illustration is linen/polyester)
flannel 34 cm × 9 cm (13½" × 3½")
lawn 34 cm × 9 cm (13½" × 3½")
1 m (1 yd) 7 mm silk ribbon in:
  yellow 15
1 m (1 yd) 4 mm silk ribbon in:
  green 33
DMC stranded cotton in:
  greens 522, 580
1 m (1 yd) bias binding to match or tone with fabric
one pearl button

Fold the strip of fabric in half. Allowing 1 cm (⅜") for seams at the cut ends, fold fabric in half again. Mark the centre of each of the four sections

Needlecase

Flowers in straight stitch, with petal stitch trumpets
Leaves and grass in straight stitch

with a pencil dot. Centre the design over the dots and work following the instructions.

When the needlecase is finished there will be four groups of daffodils along its length. When the needlecase is folded the daffodil groups are in the centre of each section.

To make up
Trim the embroidered panel to 34 cm × 9 cm (13½" × 3½"). Place it over the flannel and lawn and baste the three pieces together around the edges. Machine stitch 5 mm (³⁄₁₆") in from the edge, trim, then zig-zag over the edge.

Machine-stitch the bias binding to the edge following the previous stitching. Take care to get the rounded corners even. Press the binding towards the edge, turn over and slip-stitch with tiny stitches in matching cotton.

Turn up one end by one-quarter. This forms the pocket. Overcast the sides together with small close stitches.

An optional finish on the inside of the needlecase is the ribbon next to the binding, which is herring-boned into place.

Make a small buttonhole loop in the centre of the front edge, and sew the button in position.

Daffodils sampler

Opposite: Daffodils sewing set

Pincushion

You will need
fabric 42 cm × 18 cm (16½" × 7")
felt 40 cm × 20 cm (16" × 8")
thin batting 52 cm × 20 cm (20" × 8")
sewing cotton to match fabric
1 m (1 yd) of 7 mm silk ribbon in:
   yellow 15
1 m (1 yd) 4 mm silk ribbon in:
   green 33
DMC stranded cotton in:
   yellow 725
   greens 522, 580
84 cm (33") blind cord for piping
84 cm (33") bias binding to match fabric

Cut a strip of fabric 4 cm (1½") wide from the long side of the fabric and cut two 14 cm (5½") squares for the top and bottom of the pincushion.
   Work the daffodil motif on one square of fabric.

To make up
Make two 42 cm (16½") lengths of piping with the blind cord and the bias binding. Baste the piping in the seam position around the top and bottom panels of the pincushion, using the pattern on page 20 as a guide, then stitch either by hand or machine. It is easier to get the rounded corners even by hand.

Cut eight pieces of felt and two pieces of batting from the pattern, exactly the size of the top of the pincushion. Sew all these together, with the batting on the outside, through all thicknesses, without pulling the stitches tight. Sew a strip of batting around the sides, oversewing it to the top and bottom. Sew the embroidered top and the bottom piece to the felt and batting pad.
   Take a strip of fabric 42 cm × 4 cm (16½" × 1⅝") and press turnings on each side so that it fits the depth of the pincushion. Fit the strip firmly around the pincushion, wrong side out, pin the ends together and stitch the seam. Remove from the pincushion and press open the seam before fitting back over the pincushion, right side out, and neatly ladder-stitching it to the piping.

Scissors Holder

You will need
fabric 52 cm × 28 cm (20" × 11")
1 m (1 yd) 7 mm silk ribbon in:
   yellow 15
1 m (1 yd) 4 mm silk ribbon in:
   green 33

18

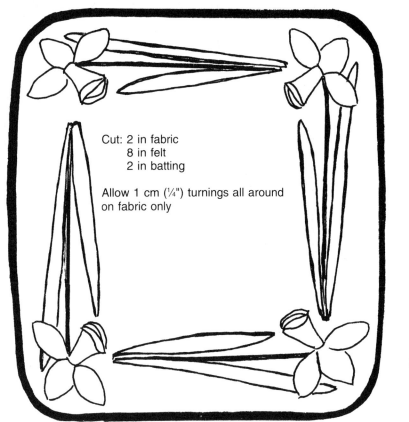

Cut: 2 in fabric
   8 in felt
   2 in batting

Allow 1 cm (¼") turnings all around
on fabric only

Pincushion

DMC stranded cotton in:
   yellow 725
   greens 522, 580
75 cm (30") bias binding to match the fabric
thin batting 52 cm × 28 cm (20" × 11")
sewing cotton to match the fabric
50 cm (18") satin ribbon to match the fabric

Cut out the pattern pieces and work the embroidery on the smallest piece. It is advisable to zig-zag or overlock around the edge first to prevent fraying.

To make up
Assemble the pieces for the pockets with the thin batting between the two layers of each piece.

Bind the straight top edges of the two pocket pieces, machining the binding to the front then turning it over and hand-stitching to the back.

Assemble the scissors case, placing the two pockets on the back piece, which also has batting between the two layers of fabric. Pin in place, then stitch all around the edge through all layers, 5 mm (³⁄₁₆") in from the edge. Trim then zig-zag or overlock. Bind the edge with the bias binding, machine-stitching it to the front, then folding over the edge and hand-stitching it to the back.

Attach a 5 cm (2") loop of satin ribbon and a small bow to the top of the scissors case.

Scissors holder

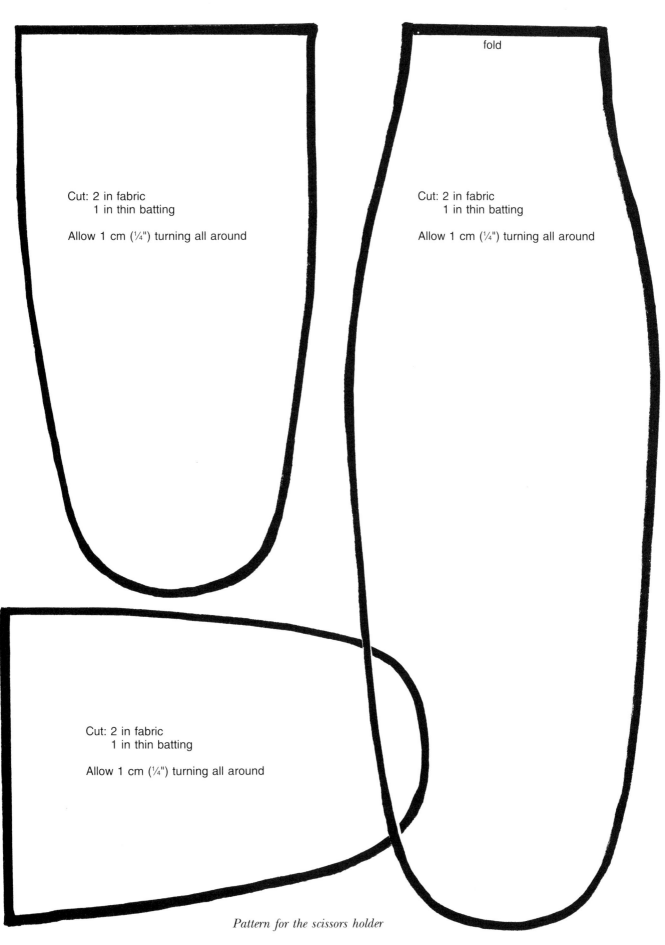

Cut: 2 in fabric
   1 in thin batting

Allow 1 cm (¼") turning all around

fold

Cut: 2 in fabric
   1 in thin batting

Allow 1 cm (¼") turning all around

Cut: 2 in fabric
   1 in thin batting

Allow 1 cm (¼") turning all around

Pattern for the scissors holder

21

Tulips

You will need
4 mm silk ribbon in:
   pinks 5, 110
DMC stranded cotton in:
   greens 470, 471

The flower stems are worked first in stem stitch with two strands of green 471. The two pink ribbons are threaded into one needle to work the flowers, which are worked in three straight stitches, starting with the centre petal. The other two stitches overlap the first one at the base of the flower. Always work from the outside into the centre.

The stitches can be spaced a little apart on some flowers to give variety, closer together in others to give the effect of a bud. The leaves are rows of stem stitch worked close together, using one strand of green 471 or 470.

Picture

You will need
3 m (3¼ yds) of 4 mm silk ribbon in:
   pinks 5, 110
DMC stranded cotton in:
   greens 470, 471
fabric 28 cm × 36 cm (11" × 14")
   (the illustration is worked on silk)
scrap of fine pale blue fabric 12 cm × 3 cm (5" × 1¼")
scrap of gold fabric about 4.5 cm (1¾") square
   (the fabrics in the illustration are blue nylon and gold organza)
stranded cottons to match the fabrics
bonding web to back the blue and gold fabrics
picture frame 22 cm × 16 cm (8¾" × 6½")
medium weight card the same size as the frame
thin batting the same size as the frame
fabric glue

Trace the shelf, bowl, flower stems and leaves only onto a piece of white paper with a medium-point black felt pen. Transfer the design by placing the

Tulips sampler

Opposite: Tulips picture

Flowers in straight stitches
Leaves and stems in stem stitch

fabric over the tracing and marking with a quilter's pencil or sharp HB pencil. If the fabric is too opaque to do this use the net method described on page 9.

Iron the small pieces of blue and gold fabric onto bonding web backed by a piece of silicone release paper or baking parchment. Cut out the shapes of the shelf and the bowl, cutting out the shelf where the bowl overlaps it. The bowl must fit exactly into the cut-out space, so take care.

Work the stems which extend down into the bowl before ironing shelf and bowl into position onto the fabric. Outline shelf and bowl with stem stitch in one strand of matching cotton.

Work the rest of the design as described on page 22.

When finished press carefully on the wrong side into a well padded surface.

To mount the picture for framing cut a piece of card to fit the frame loosely. This is to allow for the thickness of the fabric which will cover it. Cut a piece of thin batting to fit the card and lightly glue it to each corner of the card. Centre the embroidery over the card, then turn everything over carefully, face down onto a piece of clean white paper. Apply glue to one edge of the card, then turn the fabric over the edge and press down. Repeat on the opposite side, then on the other two sides. Stretch the fabric so that it fits snugly over the card, making the corners as flat and neat as possible. You may need to cut some of the fabric away from the corners. It helps to smooth the corners with a bookbinder's bone folder or flat ruler.

Still Life

Illustrated on next page; design on page 72

You will need
pale yellow cotton 30 cm × 25 cm (12" × 10")
blue cotton 30 cm × 25 cm (12" × 10")
small scraps of silk for vases
4 mm silk ribbon in:
    pinks 5, 110
    yellow 15
    mauve 23
DMC stranded cotton in:
    greens 471, 987
    colours to match the pale yellow cotton and the vases
bonding web
picture frame to fit
medium weight card
thin batting

Iron the bonding web to the back of the pale yellow and blue cottons and to the small pieces of silk. Make sure that you have a release paper between the bonding web and the iron (baking paper is good).

Cut out the arch shape from the yellow cotton, then iron the yellow cotton onto the blue cotton. Cut out the vase shapes from the silk and iron them into place.

Work a line of stem stitch in one strand of matching cotton very close to the arch shape and around the vases. Define the window sill the same way.

Work the crocuses and tulips following the instructions in the previous pages. The daffodils are a bit different, being worked with 4 mm ribbon instead of 7 mm, and having only one petal stitch for the trumpet.

Mount for framing following the instructions above for the tulip picture.

Spring Still Life (page 25)

26

SUMMER

Tiger Lilies

Illustrated on page 30

You will need
4 mm silk ribbon in:
   oranges 16, 106
DMC stranded cotton in:
   greens 581, 470
   brown 3826
DMC stranded rayon in:
   yellow R444

The stems of the spray are worked first, with two strands of green 581 in whipped chain stitch.

The flowers and buds are worked with the two orange ribbons threaded in the one needle. Use a chenille needle No. 20. Start with the central petal and make a straight stitch, leaving it a little loose. Working from the outside of the flower into the centre, make two more straight stitches on either side of the first one. Leave them loose enough to form a curve.

With two strands of brown 3826 and a No. 9 crewel needle make tiny back stitches on the petals. These stitches hold the petals in shape as well as making the spots on the lily.

The stamens are straight stitches in one strand of yellow R444 with a small back stitch in two strands of brown 3826 at the tips.

The leaves are worked in stem stitch with two strands of green 470. Work all around the outline first then fill in with parallel rows close together. To make a good point at the end of a leaf, take the

Tiger lilies sampler

needle down through the fabric at the point then come up a little behind the point and continue.

Keep the thread above the needle when working the stem stitch as this gives a finer line.

The leaves crossing behind are worked in green 581.

Curtain Tie-backs

You will need

1 metre (1 yd) of 120 cm (48") fabric (the fabric used in the illustration is a cotton/polyester furnishing satin)

50 cm (20") of medium weight interfacing

2 m (2 yds) of 4 mm silk ribbon in:
  oranges 16, 106

DMC stranded cotton in:
  greens 581, 470
  brown 3826

DMC stranded rayon in:
  yellow R444

4 brass or wooden rings 6 cm (2½") in diameter

Cut out the fabric and interfacing following the pattern. Trace the stems and leaves of the design onto a piece of white paper with a medium-tip black felt pen. If the tracing can be seen through the fabric trace it onto the fabric with a sharp HB or quilter's pencil, otherwise use the net method described on page 9.

Work the embroidery as described on page 27 on two pieces of the cut-out fabric.

To make up

Baste interfacing to the wrong side of the embroidered piece. With the lining piece and embroidered piece right sides together, machine-stitch around the edge to within 3 cm (1¼") of the narrow ends. Turn right side out and press carefully on the lining side. Turn in 1 cm (⅜") at each end, insert a ring between the two sides then ladder stitch the two ends together.

Cushion

You will need

50 cm (20") of 120 cm (48") fabric

4 m (4½ yds) of 4 mm silk ribbon in:
  oranges 16, 106

2 skeins DMC stranded cotton in:
  green 581

1 skein DMC stranded cotton in:
  green 470
  brown 3826

1 skein DMC stranded rayon in:
  yellow R444

2 m (2¼ yds) of 5 mm double-sided satin ribbon to tone with the fabric

2 m (2¼ yds) bias binding to match the fabric
  (If you wish to make piping in the same fabric as the cushion allow another 50 cm [20"])

2 m (2¼ yds) blind cord for piping

34 cm (13½") zip fastener

First cut a 36 cm (14¼") diameter circle in paper. Fold this in half and then in three. When opened out there will be six even segments to the circle. Trace the design onto the paper, aligning the sprays in the centre of each segment with the flowers to the outer edge.

Cut a piece of fabric 38 cm (15") square, place the circle of paper on this, pin securely and baste around the edge, marking each segment with an extra stitch. Transfer the design as described for the tie-backs and remove the paper, leaving the basting.

Work the sprays as in the instructions on page 27.

About 50 cm (19") from one end of the satin ribbon tie a loose bow, then pass the shorter end through the knot to make another loop. Pull the bow tight and adjust the loops so that they are all the same size, then stitch together as invisibly as possible so that the bow will not come undone. Cut the ribbon so that the two ends are each about 20 cm (8") long. Cut two 40 cm (16") lengths of ribbon. Following the photograph, arrange and pin them between the sprays so that the ribbons cross in the centre of the design. Sew down with matching cotton, using tiny stitches about 1 cm (⅜") apart at the edges of the ribbon. Pin the bow to the centre of the design then arrange, pin and sew down the two ends.

To make up

Cut out the embroidered circle, adding 1 cm (⅜") turning, and remove the basting stitches.

Cut another piece of fabric 38 cm (15") square, then cut it in half. Machine stitch together for 2.5 cm (1") at each side, then stitch the zip in the opening.

Cut the zippered fabric into a circle the same size as the other piece.

Make piping with the blind cord and bias binding. If you wish to make piping in the same fabric as the cushion cut a 5 cm (2") wide strip on the bias about 125 cm (50") long. This will probably have to be joined.

Baste the piping to the embroidered side of the cushion. Machine stitch with a piping foot.

Baste the other side of the cushion, right sides together and with the zip open, to the piped piece. It is best to have the sections of the embroidered side that are on the bias against the sections that are on the straight on the back of the cushion. Take care not to stretch the edges.

Machine stitch the two halves together, using the piping foot. Turn right side out and press carefully.

Make a pad filled with polyester batting to fit the cushion.

Stem in whipped chain stitch
Flowers in straight stitches wiith double ribbon
Stamens in straight stitch with a tiny back stitch at the end
Leaves in stem stitch

Cut: 2 in fabric
    1 in interfacing

Allow 1 cm (¼") turnings

Pattern half-size (enlarge × 2)

place on fold

Pattern for tie-back

Queen Anne's Lace

You will need
DMC perle cotton No. 5 in white
DMC stranded cotton in:
  greens 3345, 3346, 987

The stems are worked first in whipped chain with three strands of green 3345 for the main stem and two strands for the side seams.

The stalks of the flowerheads are worked in stem stitch with one strand of green 3346.

Work the flowerheads with white perle No. 5 in French knots. Some of the florets are circles of six knots with one in the centre, and others are a curved side view with three, four or five knots.

The leaves have a central stem worked in stem stitch with one strand of green 3346, with groups of three detached chains either side in two strands of green 3346 or 987. The diagram on the next page shows the arrangement of colour.

Tablecloth and Napkins

The tablecloth can be either a 120 cm (48") diameter circle or a 120 cm (48") square. The four napkins are either 30 cm (12") diameter circles or 30 cm (12") squares.

Queen Anne's lace sampler

Opposite: Tiger lilies cushion and curtain tie-backs (page 27)

You will need
150 cm (60") of 150 cm (60") wide fabric (the tablecloth and napkins in the illustration are worked
on a polyester/cotton)
2 skeins DMC perle cotton No. 5 in white
2 skeins DMC stranded cotton in:
greens 3345, 3346, 987
8 m (9 yds) white bias binding

Cut a circle of paper 27 cm (10½") in diameter. Fold
in half and then in three. When opened out the
creases will form six even segments. Trace the
design onto the paper with a black felt pen.

Pin the paper circle to the centre of the cloth and
baste around the edge, making an extra stitch at
each crease. Trace the design onto the fabric with
a quilter's pencil or sharp HB pencil. The main
stem line fits across a segment. Only the stems,
flowerhead stalks and leaf centre lines need be
traced. The rest can be embroidered freehand, any
slight variations in the flowerheads giving a freer
effect.

Work the embroidery as described on page 31.
Press the completed embroidery carefully on the
wrong side into a well padded surface.

Bind the edge of the cloth with the bias binding.

Work the napkins with the smaller motif, one to
each napkin, and bind the edges.

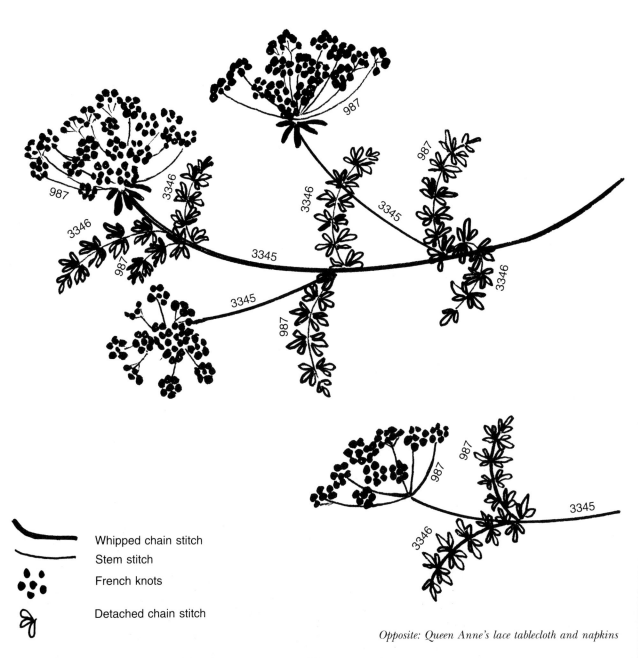

Whipped chain stitch

Stem stitch

French knots

Detached chain stitch

Opposite: Queen Anne's lace tablecloth and napkins

Lupins

You will need
4 mm silk ribbon in:
    pinks 24, 25, 103, 110, 88
    yellow 13
DMC stranded cotton in:
    greens 470, 472, 3346

The design is of three spikes of lupins, each one a slightly different combination of colours.

To start, draw three lines on the fabric for the spikes, curving the right-hand one towards the centre line. Use a quilter's pencil or sharp HB pencil.

Work each of these lines in stem stitch with one strand of green 472, then make several small detached chain stitches at the top of each spike with the same thread (see photograph).

Starting with the centre spike, make small straight stitches in pink silk ribbon 110 around and over the line of stem stitch, following the photograph. Leave space for the other colours. Then add straight stitches in yellow 13 and lastly in pink 103.

Work the other spikes in the same way, using pinks 103, 24 and 25 on one, and pinks 110 and 88 and yellow 13 on the other.

The leaves are worked in four strands of green 470 or 3346, working two detached chains one inside the other and arranging the stitches in fan shapes. Make more leaves in green 470 than in 3346.

Lupins sampler

Opposite: Lupins album cover, card and pencase

Album Cover

This design is for an album measuring 16 cm × 12.5 cm × 4 cm (6¼" × 5" × 1½").

You will need
fabric 56 cm × 20 cm (22" × 8")
lining the same size
3 m (3¼ yds) of 4 mm silk ribbon in:
  pink 110
2 m (2¼ yds) of 4 mm silk ribbon in:
  pinks 24, 25, 26, 103, 88
  yellow 13
DMC stranded cotton in:
  greens 470, 472, 3346

Fit the fabric around the album so that the short sides are inside at the spine. Crease the fabric along the edges of the album and the spine. Baste lines along the front edge and the edges of the spine. At the centre front draw three lines for the lupin spikes with a quilter's pencil or sharp HB pencil. Draw another line at the same level at the centre of the spine.

Work the embroidery as described on page 34.

To make up
Lay the lining on the embroidered fabric with right sides together. Pin or baste, then machine-stitch along the long sides and the front edge. Turn right side out and press carefully on the lining side. Turn in and slipstitch the open end.

Check the depth of the cover on the album; it should extend a fraction over the top and bottom.

Fit the cover around the album and pin at top and bottom to make the end pockets. Remove from the album and oversew the top and bottom pockets with small even stitches, in matching sewing cotton. Open the album and slip the cover over it.

Flower spikes in small straight stitches
Leaves in detached chain stitches

Bowl of Flowers

You will need

fabric 24 cm × 34 cm (9½" × 13½") (the illustration
  is worked on a furnishing polyester)

light-coloured fabric for shelf 24 cm × 3 cm (9½"
  × 1¼")

small piece of fine fabric for vase (it can be plain,
  shot or patterned as long as it tones with the
  flowers)

small amount of bonding web

2 m (2¼ yds) of 4 mm silk ribbon in:
  pink 24, 25, 26
  oranges 88, 108
  yellow 14

DMC stranded cotton in:
  greens 470, 987, 472
  brown 3826

DMC stranded rayon in:
  yellow R444

DMC perle cotton No. 8 in white

DMC perle cotton No. 5 in ecru

stranded cotton to tone with the fabric of the bowl

The strip of fabric for the shelf and the small piece
for the bowl are ironed onto the bonding web,
which must be backed with release paper or baking
parchment.

Sorbello Knot

Sorbello knot is a square stitch, named after a
town in Italy. It is best worked in a firm thread
such as perle No. 5. Following the photograph,
make a horizontal stitch along the top of the
'square', and bring the needle out in the lower
left corner of the square. Then take the needle
and thread over, then under, the initial stitch,
with the needle to the left of the thread. Take
the needle over and under the stitch again,
with the needle to the left of the thread. This
makes the knot. Pull up, then take the needle
down at the lower right corner of the square.

Sorbello knot and Queen Anne's lace sampler

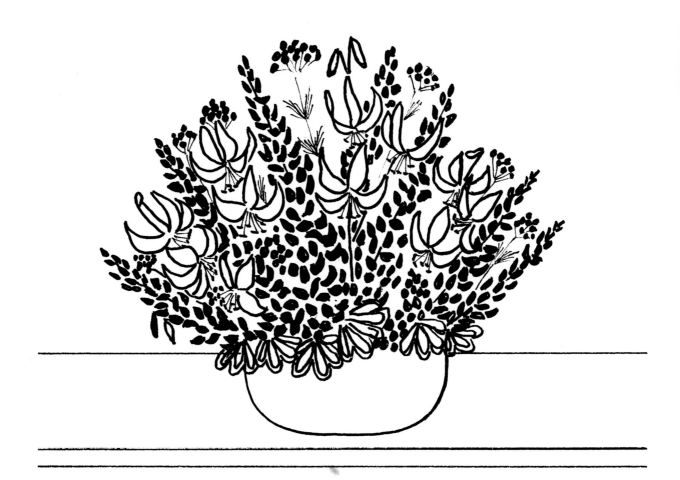

 Lupins: small straight stitches

 Queen Anne's lace: French knots
straight stitches

 Lilies: straight stitches
back stitches

 Leaves: detached chain stitches

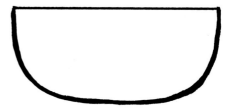

Pattern for bowl

Trace the shape of the bowl onto a piece of white paper, using a medium-tip black felt pen. Cut this out and use as a template to cut out the fabric for the bowl.

Iron the shelf strip in place on the background fabric, then iron the bowl in position over it.

Outline the top edge of the bowl with the perle No. 8, using stem stitch. Work a row of Sorbello knot stitch along the lower edge of the shelf, using perle cotton No. 5 in ecru.

Outline the bowl in stem stitch with a matching thread.

Baste an outline for the shape of the flowers. The flowers themselves can be worked freehand.

Start with the lilies, worked in the same way as described on page 27 but in different colours and slightly smaller. Use both orange ribbons threaded in one needle.

Work the lupins next, arranging them between the lilies. They are also a little smaller, otherwise worked in the same way as described on page 34.

The Queen Anne's lace is worked in perle No. 8 in white, with French knots in clusters, to fill out the design.

For the leaves at the base of the arrangement follow the instructions for the lupin leaves on page 34, but use only two strands of greens 470 or 987.

To mount the picture for framing see the instructions on page 25.

Summer Bouquet

You will need
3 m (3¼ yds) of 4 mm silk ribbon in:
    pinks 24, 25
    oranges 106, 16
2 m (2 yds) of 4 mm silk ribbon in:
    mauves 22, 23
    blue 101
    green 20
50 cm (20") of 1 cm (¼") double-sided satin ribbon
    in apricot
DMC stranded cotton in:
    pink 957
    greens 470, 471, 472
    mauve 210
    yellows 725, R444
    brown 301
    white
DMC perle cotton No. 5 in white
fabric 30 cm × 40 cm (12" × 16")

The only parts of this design which need to be transferred to the fabric are the centres of the roses, the outer stems below the bow, the lines of the stems of the lilies and the curling stems of the convolvulus. This can be done by the net method described on page 9.

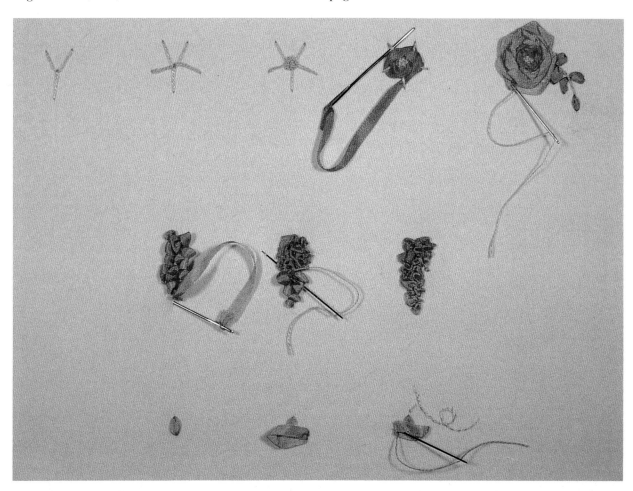

Summer Bouquet sampler   *Opposite: Summer Bouquet embroidery*

Work the spider's web roses first. Following the example in the photograph, make the groundwork in three strands of pink 957. Then work a circular cluster of French knots in two strands of yellow 725 in the centre of the groundwork.

Thread the web, starting with the deeper pink ribbon for three rows. Leave the ribbon relaxed, not tight, and twist it to get a more natural effect. Change to the lighter pink and continue till the stitches of the groundwork are covered, still leaving the ribbon fairly loose and twisted. When the rose is completed sew down to secure the loose outside petals, using one strand of pink thread. Make these stitches as invisible as possible.

For the rosebuds, make two straight stitches with both pink ribbons threaded in the needle. Add a fly stitch in two strands of green 471 outside the bud and a straight stitch onto the bud from the centre of the fly stitch.

Next work the lilies as described on page 27.

The buddleia or butterfly bush is made with small loops in the two mauve shades. Start with the deeper colour and use the paler shade near the tip of the spray, following the example in the photograph. Make a small stitch in the centre of each loop in one strand of mauve 210.

The Queen Anne's lace is worked in French knots in white perle No. 5. Add straight stitches in two strands of green 471 under the flower head and for the stems.

For the convolvulus work a small straight stitch in blue ribbon 101 (see the sample photograph). Over this make a horizontal loop of ribbon about 1 cm (¼") long. Sew the loop down at the outside edges with one strand of mauve cotton. The edges of the ribbon should meet across the centre. Make a French knot in the centre of the flower in two strands of green 472.

The convolvulus buds are a straight stitch with the ribbon twisted.

Stems are worked in stem stitch with one strand of green 472.

The rose leaves have the centre rib worked first, in two strands of green 471. Leaves in green ribbon are added each side of the centre rib, worked in small straight stitches.

The stems of the bouquet are all worked in stem stitch, using two strands and varying the greens 470, 471 and 472.

The feathery gypsophila stems are worked in fly stitches with one strand of green 471, overlapping the stitches to make small bunches. French knots in two strands of white are worked at the ends of the fly stitches.

When all the embroidery is completed tie a bow in the satin ribbon, making sure the loops are the same length, about 4 cm (1½") from the knot to the outside tip of the loop.

Pin the bow in position, turning the ribbon of the tails several times. Sew down with tiny stitches under all the folds and at the edge where necessary. The knot must be well secured with several stitches made as invisibly as possible.

Roses: spider's web, French knots in centre

Rosebud: straight stitches

Buddleia: loops

Queen Anne's lace: French knots

Lilies: straight stitches

Convolvulus: loops

Gypsophila: fly stitch + French knots

Rose leaves: stem stitch + straight stitches

AUTUMN

Dahlias

You will need
4 mm silk ribbon in:
   white 1
   reds 2, 93
   fuchsia 70
   pinks 25, 53
DMC stranded cotton in:
   yellow 725
   colours to match the ribbons
1 m (1 yd) 8 mm green double-sided satin ribbon

For each flower cut a 55 cm (21") length of ribbon.

With matching thread work running stitch in a zig-zag from side to side of the ribbon, starting with two back stitches to secure the thread. Pull the stitching up till the ribbon measures 16 cm (6½") and fasten off the thread but do not cut it. Sew the ruched ribbon down in a circle around the outside of the flower, with the cut edge to the inside. Sew down every second petal with a tiny stitch, going around the outside edge and continuing in a spiral for a second row. The rows should overlap slightly. Work in this manner until you reach the end of the ribbon, which should be at the centre of the flower. Sew the end down securely and finish off the thread.

Fill the centre with French knots in three strands of yellow 725. It usually takes six to eight knots.

Take a 5 cm (2") length of the green satin ribbon and fold it so that the two edges butt together at the centre. Fold the top of the loop over and press with the fingers. The raw edges are tucked under the edge of the flower and sewn down and the point of the leaf stitched in place.

Dahlias sampler with ribbon prepared for ruching   *Opposite: Dahlias bag*

Bag

You will need
110 cm (43") of 90 cm (36") velveteen
1 m (1 yd) of 4 mm silk ribbon in:
  white 1
  reds 2, 93
  fuchsia 70
  pinks 25, 53
DMC stranded cotton in:
  yellow 725
  colours to match the ribbons
1 m (1 yd) of 8 mm green double-sided satin ribbon
3.5 m (3¾ yds) of 3.5 cm (1½") grosgrain ribbon
110 cm (43") lining fabric
sewing cotton to match the velveteen

Cut the velveteen into one piece 58 cm × 101.5 cm (23" × 40") and one piece 20 cm (8") square. Cut the lining into matching pieces.

On the 20 cm (8") square of velveteen, which will form the pocket, mark a basting stitch for the centre of each flower of the design. Work the design following the instructions on page 44. When the embroidery is completed machine-stitch the lining to the top and bottom of the pocket, right sides together. Turn and press lightly, leaving the sides open. Baste the pocket to the centre of one side of the bag 15 cm (6") from the top. Machine-stitch the pocket at the sides and bottom.

Baste then machine-stitch the grosgrain ribbon to the bag, starting at the centre of the fabric (see diagram) and positioning it to cover the sides of the pocket. Stitch the ribbon to within 12 cm (5") of each end of the fabric, leaving 38 cm (15") loops for handles. Add another length of ribbon to the underside of the handles, for strength, and edge stitch. Stitch the handles down a further 3 cm (1½").

Stitch the lining to the top edges of the bag, right sides together. The handles must be folded away from the edge of the bag during this process. Turn

Flowers in ruched ribbon with French knot centres
Leaves in loops of satin ribbon with the ends turned
  under to form a point

right side out and press the edges, then top stitch 2.5 cm (1") from the edge.

Stitch the sides of the bag together on the right side, trim the seam and zig-zag over the edge. Turn inside out and press the seams. Stitch the seam on the inside of the bag.

From the inside, fold the lower corners to a tri-angle. Stitch across the base of the triangle 5 cm (2") from the tip. Turn the tips of the triangles to the centre of the bag and hand-stitch down. Turn the bag right side out and edge stitch the sides to define the gusset. Cut a piece of firm card 45 cm × 12 cm (17½" × 4¾"), cover with lining and insert into the bottom of the bag.

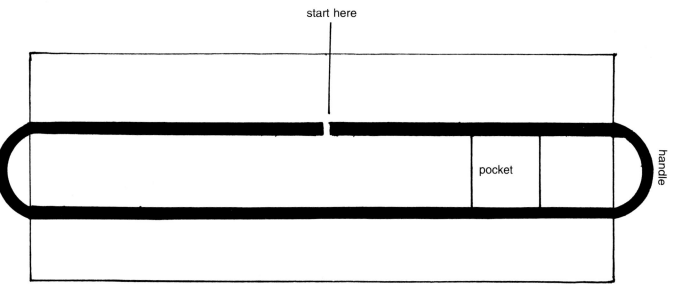

Positioning the grosgrain ribbon

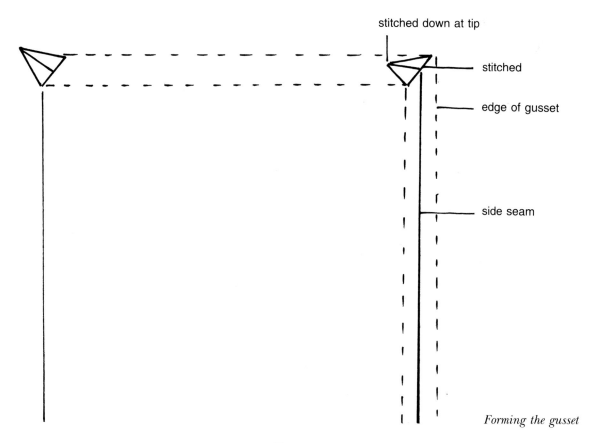

Forming the gusset

Japanese Anemones

You will need
4 mm silk ribbon in:
   pink 83
1000 denier Kanagawa silk thread in:
   greens 160, 114
   yellow 18
380 denier Kanagawa silk thread in:
   green 114

Work the centres first in satin stitch in 1000 denier green silk 114. Work two layers, the first vertical, the second horizontal. Start with a stitch in the centre, then two each side a little shorter. The second layer is worked in the same way. The result should be a smooth padded circle.

There are eight petals to each flower. Work NSEW first, then fill in between. Use the ribbon double; 40 cm (16") used double is enough for one flower.

Make tiny back stitches around the centre of the flower in 1000 denier yellow silk 18. Stems are in stem stitch using 1000 denier green silk 114. Leaves are outlined in stem stitch using either 1000 denier green silks 114 and 160.

The veins are worked in stem stitch with 380 denier green silk 114.

Jewel Box

The box illustrated is 18 cm (7⅛") square and 5 cm (2") deep. This is made from medium weight cardboard. If you don't wish to make your own box, ready-cut box kits can be bought from craft shops and the method shown here easily adapted to suit.

Japanese anemones sampler

Opposite: Japanese anemones jewel box

Flower petals in straight stitches with double ribbon
Flower centres in satin stitch surrounded by tiny back
  stitches
Stems and leaves in stem stitch

You will need

one sheet each of medium weight and light weight
cardboard (or a box kit)

50 cm (20") of 90 cm (36") fabric (the box illustrated is covered in a silk dupion, but any fairly
lightweight fabric in silk, cotton or synthetic
would be suitable; velvet or velveteen is not
suitable)

masking tape

fabric glue

sewing thread to match fabric

6 m (6½ yds) of 4 mm silk ribbon in:
pink 83

1000 denier Kanagawa silk thread in:
greens 160, 114
yellow 18

380 denier Kanagawa silk thread in:
green 114

50 cm (20") thin batting

Cut a piece of cardboard 18 cm (7¼") square for
the base and a piece 18.5 cm (7¼") square for the
lid. Cut two pieces 18.5 cm × 5 cm (7¼" × 2") for
the front and back of the box and two pieces 18 cm
× 5 cm (7¼" × 2") for the sides.

Glue the front, back and sides to the outside of
the base and cover the joins with masking tape.

Cut a piece of fabric 24 cm (9½") square. Work
the embroidery in the centre of this piece, following
the instructions on page 48.

Cut a piece of fabric 42 cm (16½") square. This
should be large enough to cover the base, come up
the sides and over onto the base on the inside.

Fit this piece, wrong side out, onto the box, taking
a triangle at each corner and pinning it up to the
top edge of the box. This must be very firm fitting.

Remove from the box and machine-stitch the
corners where they are pinned. Trim the seams to
1 cm (⅜") and press open with the fingers.

Fit over the box. It should be firm and the seams
should be exactly on the corners. Fold in the surplus
fabric at the corners so that it just fits to the corner

inside the box. Run a small amount of glue each
side of the corner inside and along the edge of the
inside base, using a large darning needle. Stretch
the fabric over the edge and down onto the base.
Work slowly, doing opposite sides.

Cover the top of the lid with a piece of batting,
glued lightly at each corner. Fold the embroidered
top over the lid, making sure it is centred. Work
over a sheet of clean white paper. If any glue gets
on the paper, change it for a clean sheet.

Glue each corner over the lid, then glue one side
followed by the side opposite, stretching the fabric
taut as you work.

Measure the inside of the box and cut two pieces
of thin cardboard a fraction smaller than the meas-
urement. Cover each piece with batting, glueing it
at each corner, then cover with fabric, making the
corners as flat and neat as possible.

Cut a piece of fabric 17.5 cm × 20 cm (7" × 8").
Turn in a small hem at the sides and fold the piece
in half lengthwise. Glue this into the back of the
box and onto the lid to form a hinge. It is best to
work with the back of the box flat on a table and
the lid butted up against it.

Cut a piece of fabric 4 cm × 6 cm (1½" × 2⅜");
fold the longer sides into the centre then fold up
in half. Slip-stitch the sides and glue to centre front
of the lid to make a tab. Glue the lid lining in place.

The lining for the base can now be slipped into
place. If it is a little loose, put a small dab of glue
at each corner.

Notes on box-making

Always measure accurately and ensure corners are
absolutely square. Never cut card for lining until the
outside of the box is completed.

Use as little glue as possible and spread it with a
large darning needle.

Check at every stage to make sure everything is
correct before going on to the next stage.

Work on clean scrap paper, changing it at every
stage.

Michaelmas Daisies

The small dainty asters portrayed here are usually called Michaelmas daisies in the northern hemisphere and Easter daisies in the southern hemisphere.

You will need
4 mm silk ribbon in:
   mauves 70, 84, 23
   pink 144
DMC stranded cotton in:
   yellow 725
   green 367

Each flower is composed of 20 petals worked in straight stitch. Work NSEW first, leaving a space in the centre, then add four petals to each segment.

Fill the centre with French knots in three strands of yellow 725.

The leaves are in detached chain stitch with a straight stitch in the centre, worked with two strands of green 367.

Half-open flowers are made with several straight stitches coming in to a point, with three small detached chains worked over the point in one strand of green 367.

Blouse

Choose a simple style, whether it's one to make up or ready made. If you are making the blouse yourself, work the embroidery on the cut-out front section before making up.

The design can be transferred either by laying the fabric over the design and tracing with a quilter's pencil or sharp HB pencil, or by the net method described on page 9.

You will need
1.5 m (1½ yds) silk ribbon in:
   mauves 23, 70, 84
   pink 144
DMC stranded cotton in:
   green 367
   yellow 725

Work the design following the instructions above.

Make sure that the ribbons are well sewn down on the back. This is very important on a garment or any article that is going to be used and washed.

Press the embroidery carefully on the wrong side into a well padded surface and make up.

Michaelmas daisies sampler

Opposite: Michaelmas daisies blouse

mauve 23

mauve 70

pink 144

mauve 23

mauve 84

pink 144

mauve 23

mauve 70

mauve 84

pink 144

mauve 23

pink 144

mauve 84

mauve 23

pink 144

pink 144

mauve 70

Flowers in straight stitch with French knot centres
Leaves in detached chain stitch

Basket of Flowers

Illustrated on page 56

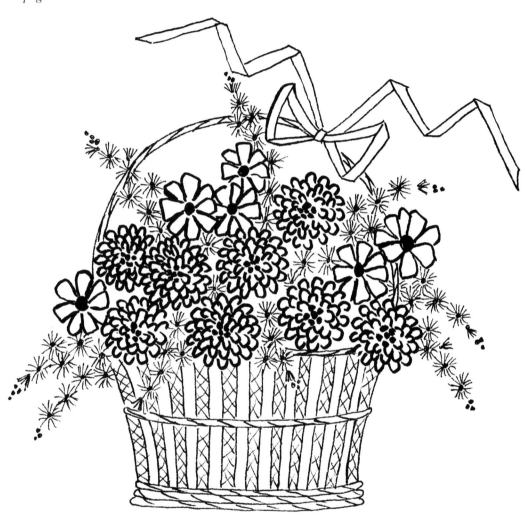

Anemone: straight stitches with
satin stitch centre

Dahlia: ruched ribbon with
French knot centre

Michaelmas daisy: straight stitches, French
knot centre and buds

Basket: herringbone stitch over satin ribbon

Basket base and handle: twisted
satin ribbon

Basket of Flowers

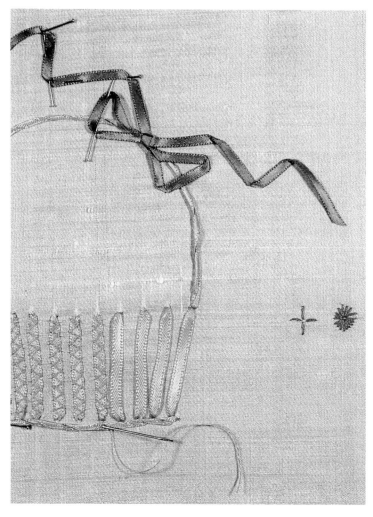

You will need
2 m (2¼ yds) of 4 mm silk ribbon in:
    mauve 145
    pinks 152, 144
3 m (3¼ yds) of 4 mm silk ribbon in:
    pink 83
1 m (1 yd) of 3 mm double-sided satin ribbon in:
    pale green
50 cm (20") of 3 mm double-sided satin ribbon in:
    darker green
DMC stranded cotton in:
    mauves 210, 553
    yellow 725
    greens 470, 472 and to match the satin ribbons

Transfer only the design of the basket to the fabric. Either trace directly onto the fabric with a sharp HB pencil or transfer the design by the net method described on page 9.

Trace only a single line for each strut of the basket and for the handle. Mark the centres of the larger flowers. The rest can be worked freehand.

Make long, fairly loose stitches in pale green satin ribbon for the struts. Work herringbone stitch over the ribbon with one strand of matching cotton. When all the struts are completed bring the ribbon out at one side of the base, twist it fairly tightly and either hold with one hand or pin. Sew down with a small stitch between each twist. Repeat for three rows at the base, a single row halfway up the basket and another at the top edge, and also for the handle.

Work the dahlias next as described on page 44, then the anemones as on page 48.

The sprays of Michaelmas daisies in this design are worked in straight stitches in stranded cotton rather than ribbon, using two strands of mauve 210 or 553 and 16 stitches for each flower. Work NSEW first then fill in.

A French knot in two strands of yellow 725 makes the centre of each flower. The tiny buds are worked in two strands of green 470 or 472.

Basket of Flowers sampler

Stems are added inside the basket between the struts, using stem stitch with two strands. Both greens are used, with the darker one predominating.

Tie a bow in the darker satin ribbon and pin out on the basket handle. Stitch in the folds with matching thread.

To mount for framing see the instructions on page 25.

WINTER

Hellebore (Winter Rose)

The technique used for this flower is shadow quilting. This consists of two layers of a transparent fabric with a design cut out of another fabric sandwiched between the layers and stitched around with back stitch.

It is helpful to back the fabric for the design with a bonding web before cutting out the design. After it is cut out it can be ironed onto the bottom layer of fabric.

Lampshade

You will need

a covered lampshade similar to the one in the illustration, which is 30.5 cm (12") in diameter at the bottom

60 cm (24") of 90 cm (36") transparent fabric (the fabric in the illustration is polyester georgette)

opaque fabric 30 cm × 20 cm (12" × 8") for the design

bonding web the same size

1000 denier Kanagawa silk thread in:
   pink 190
   greens 114, 160
fabric glue
2 m (2¼ yds) lace or braid

Iron the bonding web onto the opaque fabric, making sure that there is a silicon release paper between the iron and the bonding web. Baking paper is ideal.

Trace the design onto the bonded fabric with a sharp pencil and cut out.

Make a paper pattern of the lampshade. This is most easily done by rolling the lampshade over a large sheet of paper and marking the edges as you go. Start at the seam.

Hellebore sampler

Opposite: Hellebore lampshade

58

Flowers, leaves and stems in shadow quilting
Centres in bullion stitch

60

Cut out the pattern allowing 2.5 cm (1") turnings all around. Mark the grain line in the centre.

Cut two pieces of transparent fabric from the pattern, ensuring that the centre of the lampshade is on the straight grain of the fabric. Zig-zag or over-lock the edges of each piece.

Place the cut-out design in the centre of one piece of fabric and iron it on.

Place the other piece of fabric over this and baste the layers together vertically every 5 cm (2"), taking care not to stretch the fabric.

Use a 20 cm (8") ring frame for the embroidery.

Work the flowers first, using back stitch in the pink silk to outline the petals. Stitch close to the outline. Then work the centre ribs of the leaves in running stitch in green 114, followed by the outlines of the leaves in back stitch in the same silk.

The centres of the flowers are worked in bullion stitch in green 160, making six turns around the needle for each stitch.

To make up

Carefully press the embroidery on the wrong side into a well padded surface.

Place the embroidered fabric around the lampshade, wrong side out, and pin the seam. It should fit firmly and not be distorted.

Make sure that there is the same amount of turning above and below the shade.

Machine-stitch the seam, trim and press.

Fit the cover over the lampshade, right side out.

Run a little fabric glue along the inside edges of the top and bottom of the original lampshade. Turn the edge of the embroidered fabric over the edges so that it is glued to the lampshade. Start at the centre front, top edge, then the corresponding point at the bottom edge. Pull firmly to get a smooth finish and gradually work round the shade to the back. Try to pull on the straight grain of the fabric.

Stitch the lace or braid to the edges of the lampshade.

Poinsettias

You will need
50 cm (20") of 4 mm silk ribbon for each flower in:
  red 2
DMC stranded cotton in:
  green 470
  yellow 725
  red 666

Each petal is worked with two or three straight stitches. Work the centre stitch first then bring up the needle just a little under the point of the petal and make the next stitch. If necessary add another stitch the other side of the centre stitch.

The petals of the poinsettia are not all the same size so it is appropriate to vary them.

With one strand of red 666 make a small fly stitch at the tip of each petal and one or two tiny stitches to hold the petals together.

The centres are worked with three strands of yellow 725 in small detached chain stitches. Work around the edge of the centre first, then fill in.

The centre ribs of the leaves are worked first, in stem stitch with three strands of green 470.

Fly stitch, also with three strands of the same green, is worked for the leaf outlines. Start at the base of the leaf and make one side of the fly stitch longer than the other. Work two rows.

Table Centre

You will need
fabric 45 cm (18") square (the fabric used in the illustration is a polyester linen look)
10 m (11 yds) of 4 mm silk ribbon in:
  red 2
3 skeins DMC stranded cotton in:
  green 470
1 skein DMC stranded cotton in:
  yellow 725
  red 666

Cut a circle 42 cm (16½") in diameter from the fabric and zig-zag or overlock the edge in matching machine cotton.

Poinsettias sampler

Opposite: Poinsettias table centre

Fold the circle in four and mark each quarter with a pin.

Place the fabric over the design so that the design fits across one quarter.

Trace the petals and centre ribs of the leaves onto the fabric with a sharp pencil. It is not necessary to trace the outlines of the leaves as these can be worked freehand very easily once the centre ribs have been embroidered.

Trace the design in the other three quarters.

Work the design following the instructions on page 62.

To finish

A simple and very easy finish is to turn the edge over once and with three strands of green 470 make large overcasting stitches around the cloth. When the circle is completed, work back the other way so that there is a V on the front of the hem. Otherwise bind the edge with bias binding in green or red.

Flowers in straight stitch with fly stitch points, chain stitch centres
Leaves in fly stitch with stem stitch ribs

One quarter of the design

Snowdrops

You will need
4 mm silk ribbon in:
  white 3
  green 33
DMC stranded cotton in:
  white
  greens 988, 3363

For each flower start with three small loops in white silk ribbon, each about 5 mm (¼") long. With one strand of white cotton put a tiny stitch in the underside of each loop to attach it to the fabric, then work two fly stitches at the end of the loops with one strand of green 988, as in the photograph.

Next work the three petals over the loops, starting at the centre a little above the loops. Make two straight stitches, one over the other, for each petal. Work the side petals first, the centre one last. Using one strand of white make tiny stitches where the petals meet the loops. Sometimes a stitch is needed at the outside of the petals too. These stitches should be nearly invisible.

Work three satin stitches in three strands of green 988 at the base of each flower, then stem stitch in one strand of the same green for the little stem.

The main stems are worked in whipped chain stitch in three strands of green 3363, with two straight stitches where the main stem joins the fine stem.

Snowdrops sampler

Leaves are formed with long straight stitches in green ribbon 33, held down with running stitches down the centres in one strand of green 3363. The running stitches are long on the surface and short underneath.

Waistcoat

You will need

pattern and fabric for a plain waistcoat (the illustration is worked in grey velveteen, but firm wool, silk or cotton would also be suitable)

7 m (7¾ yds) of 4 mm silk ribbon in:
  white 3
2 m (2¼ yds) of 4 mm silk ribbon in:
  green 33
50 cm (20") of 1 cm (¼") satin ribbon in:
  pale blue
pale blue cotton to match the satin ribbon
DMC stranded cotton in:
  white
  greens 988, 3363

Cut out the waistcoat pattern. The bunch of snowdrops is placed high on the left front of the waistcoat before making up the garment.

As a guide for the embroidery, trace the spray onto tissue paper, just marking a dot at the top of each flower and marking in the stems. Do not mark the leaves or the bow as these can easily be worked freehand.

Pin the tracing in position and baste what is marked with small stitches in white cotton. Then tear away the tissue paper. (Baking paper can be used instead of tissue if you like; it tears away very easily.)

Work the flowers first, then the stems, then the leaves, which may have to be threaded under some of the flowers.

Velveteen cannot be put in a ring frame because it will mark, so take care not to pull the stitches too tight when you are working, particularly the whipped chain stitch.

Lastly tie a bow with the satin ribbon and pin out in place. Stitch the bow down with tiny stitches about every 1.5 cm (½") along each side of the ribbon.

When the embroidery is completed press carefully on the wrong side into a well padded surface, then make up the waistcoat. This design would also be suitable for a cushion or a bag.

Opposite: Snowdrops waistcoat

Flowers in loops, straight stitches and fly stitches with satin stitch bases
Leaves in straight stitch with running stitch
Stems in whipped chain stitch

Christmas Wreath

The wreath is made up of poinsettias, snowdrops and hellebore. The snowdrops and hellebores are worked differently to those in the previous designs as the scale is smaller. The addition of stitches in gold thread and gold beads gives a festive sparkle to the wreath.

You will need
fabric 36 cm (14") square (the wreath in the illustration is worked on silk dupion)
3 m (3¼ yds) of 4 mm silk ribbon in:
 red 175
DMC stranded cotton in:
 red 304
 greens 3345, 986, 470
 yellow 3820
 white
DMC *Fil Or* (gold thread)
small piece medium weight Vilene
small quantity tiny gold beads

Cut a 16 cm (6½") diameter circle out of paper and fold in four. Open out and place in the centre of the fabric. Draw around it with a sharp pencil. Mark the four quarters as indicated by the creases, aligning them NSEW on the fabric.

The quarter points are the centres of the poinsettias.

You shouldn't need to mark in much more than the centres of the poinsettias and pencil dots to indicate the fan of flowers above the poinsettias, as most of this design can be worked freehand. Don't draw in the centre ribs of the poinsettia leaves until you have worked the poinsettia flowers.

Cut a semi-circle of paper to use as a guide to place the fan shapes above the poinsettias.

Start with the poinsettias and work the flowers following the instructions on page 62. The leaves, however, are worked in two strands of green 3345, making three fly stitches at each point of the leaf.

The snowdrops are next. First work the stems in one strand of green 986, following the curve of the main circle and varying the length of the stems. The flowers are worked in two strands of white in small detached chain stitches. With two strands of green 986 make a French knot at the base of each flower and add lines of stem stitch for leaves.

Christmas wreath sampler   *Opposite: Christmas wreath*

Each bunch of snowdrops will look a little different, which adds to the charm of the design.

The hellebores are cut out of the Vilene. Draw them on the Vilene first with a sharp pencil. They are sewn in place with one strand of green 470, making a straight stitch between each petal to the centre of the flower. Sew three gold beads into the centre of each flower.

The fan shapes are worked in two strands of green 470, using detached chain stitches with long tails. Add another chain stitch in gold thread around the green one but in the other direction.

To mount for framing see the instructions on page 25.

Poinsettia: straight stitch with fly stitch tips, detached chain stitch centres

Leaves: fly stitch with stem stitch ribs

Hellebore: Vilene with straight stitches and beads at centre

Snowdrops: detached chain stitches
with a French knot at the base

Stems and leaves: stem stitch

Fans: chain stitches with a long tail
surrounded by another detached
chain stitch worked in the other direction

71

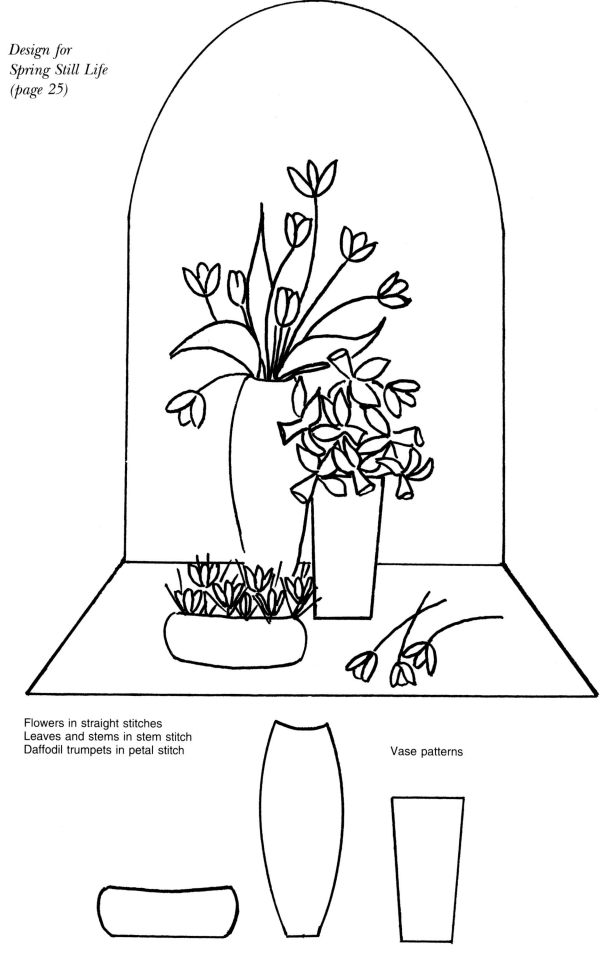

Design for
Spring Still Life
(page 25)

Flowers in straight stitches
Leaves and stems in stem stitch
Daffodil trumpets in petal stitch

Vase patterns